New READING 360 PLAYS



# Sir Gawain and the Green Knight

Steve Barlow and Steve Skidmore



**Illustrated by**
Bethan Matthews

**Series Editors**
Steve Barlow and Steve Skidmore

# Sir Gawain and the Green Knight

The scene is a school stage, where Ms Clarke's Drama Group are rehearsing their production of *Sir Gawain and the Green Knight*. It isn't a very good stage. It's a bit rickety, the curtains are worn, the lights (if any) don't work very well – in fact, it's probably quite a lot like your school stage. Ms Clarke is determined to impress Mrs Phillips, the Head Teacher, who doesn't really approve of drama. The Drama Group is determined to have fun.

## The Characters

| Members of the Drama Group | | Characters in the play |
|---|---|---|
| Sean | *plays* | **The Minstrel** |
| Barry | *plays* | **Sir Gawain** |
| Sam | *plays* | **The Green Knight** |
| Rowena | *plays* | **King Arthur** |
| Katie | *plays* | **Queen Guinevere** |
| Joseph | *plays* | **The Lord of the Castle** |
| Alison | *plays* | **The Lady of the Castle** |
| Kieran | *plays* | **The Guide** |
| Ms Clarke (Teacher) | | |
| **Non-speaking parts** | | |
| Lee | *plays* | **The Giant** |
| Billy | *plays* | **The Dragon** |
| Other children | *play* | **Knights and Ladies at King Arthur's Court and Knights and Ladies at the Lord of the Castle's Court** |
| Jason (Stage Manager) | | |

***Mrs Phillips**, the Head Teacher, does not appear. We have to imagine that she is sitting in the audience. Whenever Ms Clarke addresses Mrs Phillips, she speaks to the audience.*

*Sir Gawain and the Green Knight* is a play about putting on a play. This means that all the actors in the play must play two characters:

- a member of the Drama Group
- the character he or she is playing

For instance, the actor who is playing King Arthur also plays Rowena.

Before you read the play, write a sketch for each pair of characters.

**Actor's name:** ____________________________________________

**Member of the Drama Group: Rowena**

Rowena is a bit of a bully (she has swapped parts with Brian, who is too frightened to refuse).

**Character in the play: King Arthur**

King Arthur is a wise king, but a bit hot-headed. He loves a good story.

**Scene 1**
*The school stage is set as a chamber in King Arthur's castle. If you have a curtain, it should be closed at the beginning.*

**Ms Clarke:** *(Offstage)* Well, I can't help it if King Arthur's crown is coming apart. Use some sticky tape or something.

**Barry:** *(Offstage)* Please, Miss, can I go to the ...

**Ms Clarke:** *(Offstage)* No, you can't. I'm sorry, but we're just about to start. You should have gone before.

*(Ms Clarke comes to the front of the stage, looking flustered. She speaks to the audience where Mrs Phillips is supposedly sitting.)*

**Ms Clarke:** Oh, Mrs Phillips, I'm so glad you could come to our final dress rehearsal. I know the Drama Group has been in a bit of hot water lately, what with the angels fighting the shepherds during the Nativity play, but we've all worked really hard this time.

*(There is a loud crash offstage. Ms Clarke turns round.)*

**Ms Clarke:** *(Shouting)* Barry! Stop that! Put the sword down!

**Barry:** *(Offstage)* Sorry, Miss.

**Ms Clarke:** *(Talking to Mrs Phillips)* Er, sorry about that. I'll just introduce the play and then we'll 'take it away', as they say.

*(Ms Clarke coughs nervously.)*

**Ms Clarke:** Good evening, ladies and gentlemen, and welcome to our Drama Group's presentation of the story of 'Sir Gawain and the Green Knight'. *(She waits. Nothing happens.)*

**Ms Clarke:** *(Whispers loudly)* Jason – that's your cue.

*(The play begins. The curtain jerks open. The actors aren't ready and have to scamper to their places. King Arthur's crown has been stuck together in a hurry and not very well.)*

**Ms Clarke:** Scene One – King Arthur's Court.

*(She leaves the stage and goes to sit beside Mrs Phillips.)*

**The Minstrel:** It was Christmas time in King Arthur's court. On New Year's Day, all the nobbly knights ...

**Ms Clarke:** *(Whispers loudly)* 'Noble' knights!

**The Minstrel:** ... noble knights and ladies were gathered for a great feast. But King Arthur would not allow the feast to start until he had heard a wonderful story, or seen a great marvel.

**King Arthur:** You knights and ladies in my hall,
Have you no tales to tell ...?

**Ms Clarke:** Rowena, why are you playing King Arthur? It's supposed to be Brian.

**Rowena:** We did a swap, Miss. *(Dangerously)* Brian doesn't mind, do you, Brian?

*(Brian quickly shakes his head.)*

**Ms Clarke:** Oh, all right, get on with it.

**King Arthur:** Have you no tales to tell
Of daring deeds, and battles brave
With giants and dragons fell?

Miss, what does 'fell' mean?

**Ms Clarke:** You mustn't stop a dress rehearsal to ask questions, Rowena. Anyway, I've explained it before. It means 'dangerous and wicked'. Go on, Sean.

**The Minstrel:** Suddenly, there came a sound of horse's hooves. Everyone turned to stare as the doors of the hall burst open, and in strode a monstrous figure!

*(The Green Knight comes in, making 'clip-clop' noises with a pair of coconut shells.)*

**Ms Clarke:** Sam! You're supposed to leave your coconut shells offstage!

**Sam:** Sorry, Miss.

**Ms Clarke:** *(To Mrs Phillips, as Sam takes the coconut shells off.)* She's a bit forgetful, Mrs Phillips. I know the Green Knight should be played by a boy really, but Sam's very tall, and she is one of our best actors.

*(The Green Knight returns, carrying an axe).*

**The Minstrel:** In came a huge figure, a terrible giant of a man, armed with a great, sharp axe, and all dressed in green.

**The Green Knight:** I challenge all King Arthur's court,
You worthy knights of fame,
To play with me, here in this hall,
A merry Christmas game.

**The Minstrel:** The knights and ladies were all amazed. The Green Knight bowed to the King, and said:

**The Green Knight:** King Arthur, take this axe from me,
And strike with might and main,
For if you strike me hard enough,
I'll never rise again!

But if I should survive your blow,
A promise you must make:
To seek me out one year from now,
An answering blow to take.

**The Minstrel:** Then King Arthur grew angry, and went to take the axe from the Green Knight. But Sir Gawain spoke up:

**Sir Gawain:** My Lord, you must not risk your life.
I claim it as my right
To undertake the challenge of
This strange, enchanted knight.

**The Minstrel:** Then Sir Gawain took the axe. The Green Knight bowed his head ...

*(The Green Knight stands with his back to the audience and his head bowed.)*

**The Minstrel:** ... and Sir Gawain swung the sharp axe, and cut through the Green Knight's neck so that his head rolled on the floor.

*(For safety, Gawain must aim his blow in front of the Green Knight's head. If the Green Knight's back is to the audience, they will not be able to tell that the blow is aimed to miss. The Green Knight pulls his head back inside his costume, and one of the ladies lifts her skirt to reveal a green football with a face painted on it.)*

**The Minstrel:** The frightened knights and ladies kicked at the head as it rolled on the floor ...

*(The knights and ladies get carried away. A game of football starts.)*

**Lee:** On my head!

*(He heads the 'head' into the audience. Ms Clarke has to bring it back.)*

**Ms Clarke:** You can't head a head, Lee, you silly boy.

*(She gives the 'head' back to the Green Knight.)*

**The Minstrel:** The knights and ladies watched in terror as the Green Knight stood, and picked up his head.

**The Green Knight:** My home is the Green Chapel.
In one year, we shall see
If you are brave enough to come
And take a blow from me.

*(Lee creeps up behind him and waggles the 'head' from behind.)*

**Lee:** Gig us a gottle of geer.

**Ms Clarke:** Lee! One more piece of silliness and I shan't allow you to be in the play!

**The Minstrel:** And so the Green Knight strode from the court, and King Arthur turned to Sir Gawain ...

**King Arthur:** Gawain, a great adventure
Has begun for you today,
But what it means is more than you,
And more than I, can say.

**Scene 2**
*The scene is the same as that in Scene 1. Ms Clarke stands to address the audience.*

**Ms Clarke:** Scene Two – King Arthur's court, one year later.

**The Minstrel:** Spring, summer and autumn had come and gone. On All Saints' Day, Sir Gawain set off on his great horse, Gringolet, to find the Green Chapel and keep his bargain with the Green Knight.

*(Sir Gawain enters. King Arthur, Queen Guinevere and all the knights and ladies gather to see him go. Everyone is very sad.)*

**The Minstrel:** Queen Guinevere spoke up, and said ...

**Guinevere:** My brave knight, dear Gawain,
I pray that you may safely go,
And safe return again.

*(Gawain leaves the stage and the sound of hoofbeats can be heard. Arthur, Guinevere and the knights and ladies leave the stage. Jason, the Stage Manager, brings on a withered bush in a pot.)*

**The Minstrel:** Gringolet's hooves struck sparks from the stones as Sir Gawain rode away from his friends. He did not think he would ever come back. His journey was full of danger. He had to fight boars, and bulls, and bears. Once, he fought a dragon ...

*(A dragon comes on and Gawain fights it. It is a rather odd-looking dragon with a cardboard box head and eggbox teeth, and its body is a sheet with several people underneath. While the fight goes on, Ms Clarke whispers to Mrs Phillips.)*

**Ms Clarke:** The Art Group made the dragon when we did Chinese New Year, so it's not quite right, but I didn't think anyone would mind.

*(Gawain defeats the dragon which staggers off, mortally wounded.)*

**The Minstrel:** Wolves and wild men attacked Gawain, and he had to fight a terrifying giant.

*(The Giant comes on. He is played by the smallest member of the Drama Group. He and Gawain fight.)*

**Ms Clarke:** *(To Mrs Phillips)* Oh, dear ... he does look a bit silly, doesn't he? But he really wanted to be in the play.

*(Gawain wounds the Giant, who staggers offstage to die.)*

**The Minstrel:** The winter was hard. Half-dead with the cold, Gawain rode on. He began to think he would never find the Green Chapel. Then, on Christmas Eve, while he was riding through a dark forest, he saw a mighty castle rising up before him.

**Sir Gawain:** The Green Knight I must find, before
The ending of the year.
Perhaps this castle's lord will know
If he lives somewhere near.

**The Minstrel:** So Sir Gawain knocked on the door, and the Lord of the Castle came out to greet him.

*(Jason takes the bush offstage. The scene is now the courtyard of the Lord's Castle. Gawain and the Lord greet each other with lots of handslapping and greetings in the latest style.)*

**Ms Clarke:** That's quite enough, you two. A simple handshake will do nicely.

**The Minstrel:** The Lord of the Castle was overjoyed to see Gawain, and invited him to the Christmas feast.

**The Lord of the Castle:** Your fame has come before you, sir.
Now, welcome to my hall!
The bravest of King Arthur's knights
Does honour to us all.

**The Minstrel:** Sir Gawain would have liked to spend Christmas in the warm and splendid hall of this kind Lord. But he knew he could not stay.

**Sir Gawain:** The Green Knight I have promised
To meet on New Year's Day,
But though I have searched hard and long,
I cannot find the way.

**The Lord of the Castle:** *(Laughing)* Then you may stay and rest with us
Without the slightest fear.
The Chapel of the Knight you seek
Lies just two miles from here!

**The Minstrel:** Sir Gawain was overjoyed to hear that he was near the end of his journey. The Lord of the Castle promised to send a guide to lead him to the Green Chapel in time to meet the Green Knight.

*(The knights and ladies of the Lord's Court come on to the stage and dance as the Minstrel continues.)*

**The Minstrel:** For the three days of Christmas, the Lord of the Castle and his Lady feasted and made merry, and Sir Gawain was very happy to be with such good friends. Before they went to bed on the last day, the Lord said to Gawain:

**The Lord of the Castle:** Tomorrow, while I go to hunt,
You rest here in my hall,
And everything I catch, I swear
That you shall have it all.

And everything that comes to you
You must pass on to me!
Who'll win most from this Christmas game?
That, we shall have to see.

**The Minstrel:** Gawain wasn't sure what the Lord of the Castle meant by this, but he agreed to play the strange game.

*(The Lord and Lady of the Castle and the knights and ladies of the court say goodnight to Gawain and leave the stage. Gawain lies down to sleep.)*

**Scene 3**
*Inside the Lord's Castle.*

**Ms Clarke:** Scene Three – The Lord's Castle.

**The Minstrel:** The next morning, the Lord of the Castle rode out before dawn. Gawain lay asleep, until he heard his door open, and the Lady of the Castle came in.

**The Lady of the Castle:** Ah, now I've caught you, Sir Gawain,
I'll never let you go again!

**Sir Gawain:** My lady, what? How can this be?
Whatever can you want from me?

**The Lady of the Castle:** Be still, for all my pleasure is
To speak with you, and steal a ...

Miss! Do I have to?

**Ms Clarke:** Yes, Alison. It's in the story.

**The Lady of the Castle:** You said I didn't have to while we were practising.

**Ms Clarke:** But this is the dress rehearsal, Alison. You've got to do it some time.

**The Lady of the Castle:** But, Miss, it's Barry!

**Sir Gawain:** *(Dropping out of character)* What's wrong with me?

**The Lady of the Castle:** Do you want a list?

**Ms Clarke:** You don't *really* have to kiss him, Alison, it just has to look as if you are kissing him.

**The Lady of the Castle:** I'd rather kiss a slug.

**Ms Clarke:** Alison!

**The Lady of the Castle:** Oh, all right.

*(She kisses the air a good thirty centimetres from Sir Gawain's cheek, looking as if she is sucking a lemon.)*

**The Minstrel:** When the Lord of the Castle returned that evening, he brought the antlers of a fine stag he had caught while out hunting, and gave them to Gawain.

*(The Lord of the Castle enters with a pair of Christmas 'Rudolph' foam antlers and gives them to Sir Gawain.)*

**The Lord of the Castle:** Now I have kept my promise
With the antlers of this deer,
And you must give me everything
That you've been given here.

*(Gawain hesitates.)*

**Ms Clarke:** Go on, Barry!

*(Barry kisses the air a long way from the Lord's cheek.)*

**The Lord of the Castle:** Ugh! Gross!

**Ms Clarke:** *(Fiercely)* Stick to the script!

*(During the next speech, Gawain and the Lord and Lady of the Castle act out their parts in silence.)*

**The Minstrel:** The next day, the same thing happened. The Lady of the Castle kissed Sir Gawain, once when they met, and again when they parted. When the Lord of the Castle came back from the hunt, he gave Gawain the head of a great boar he had killed, and Gawain gave him two kisses in return. But on the third day ...

*(The Lord of the Castle leaves the stage. The Lady of the Castle takes the belt from her costume and gives it to Gawain.)*

**The Lady of the Castle:** I have for you this magic belt.
It carries a great charm,
For anyone who puts it on
Shall never come to harm.

**The Minstrel:** Sir Gawain thought, if I wear that belt, the Green Knight can strike as hard as he likes, and he will not be able to kill me. So he took the belt and the Lady of the Castle kissed him three times.

*(The Lord of the Castle enters, holding a moth-eaten bit of fur.)*

**The Lord of the Castle:** See, I have brought a fine fox brush.
What have you got for me?

*(Gawain 'kisses' the Lord of the Castle three times.)*

**The Lord of the Castle:** I've won the most from this day's sport,
That I can clearly see!
The hour is late. You must prepare;
The Knight in Green awaits.
Tomorrow, at the Chapel Green
Gawain shall meet his fate.

**Scene 4**
*The Green Chapel. It is not really a chapel, but a deep valley, where dark rocks are covered with rotting plants. The splashing of a stream can be heard.*

**Ms Clarke:** Scene Four – The Green Chapel.

**The Minstrel:** The next morning, Sir Gawain set off before sunrise. His guide led him to a dark and gloomy valley. Then he stopped and said:

**The Guide:** Good sir, the knight you go to meet
Is deadly, strong and cruel.
Leave, while you can! I'll never tell.
Go, sir! Don't be a fool.

**Sir Gawain:** My life is precious to me, but
My honour is more dear.
Gawain may die, but none shall say
He ran away from fear.

*(The Guide bows and leaves the stage.)*

**The Minstrel:** So saying, Sir Gawain rode into the valley to meet the terrible Green Knight.

*(The Green Knight enters, carrying his axe.)*

**The Green Knight:** Ah, welcome, sir! You've kept your word,
So now come here and kneel.
This time it is my turn to strike;
My sharp axe you shall feel.

*(Gawain kneels with his back to the audience. The Green Knight prepares to strike, lifts his axe, and brings it down (see note on page 10), but Gawain cannot help crouching lower and the Green Knight stops the blade before it touches his neck.)*

**The Green Knight:** You moved! You flinched! You're not Gawain!
For courage you do lack!

**Sir Gawain:** Forgive me; if my head's cut off,
I cannot put it back.

*(The Green Knight prepares to deliver a second blow. This time, Gawain does not flinch, but the Green Knight still pulls the axe up before it strikes.)*

**The Green Knight:** That's better! I see you have found
Your courage now, my friend.

**Sir Gawain:** Don't waste your time with threats!

**The Green Knight:** Why, then, it's time to make an end.

*(The Green Knight prepares to deliver a third blow. The axe falls this time, but only cuts Gawain's neck on the side. Gawain jumps aside, holding his neck, and draws his sword.)*

**Sir Gawain:** Now I have kept my promise, sir,
And you have done your worst;
But if you wish another blow,
You'll have to fight me first!

**The Green Knight:** Now why are you so angry, sir?
For what am I to blame?
I've kept my promises to you ...
But have you done the same?

**Sir Gawain:** I don't know what you mean, sir.

**The Green Knight:** No? You're a forgetful man.
Where is the belt my wife gave you?
Deny it if you can!

**Sir Gawain:** Your wife?

**The Green Knight:** I am your host, the Lord
Whose castle you have seen.
By magic I can turn myself
Into the Knight in Green.

To test your worth, I challenged you
To play my Christmas game.
The first day, my wife kissed you, and
You paid me back the same.

The second day, two kisses;
On the third day, kisses three;
But there was something else she gave,
You did not give to me.

*(The Green Knight points at the belt Gawain was given by the Lady of the Castle.)*

**The Green Knight:** So, twice the axe did you no harm.
It was not so the third.
It wounded you upon the neck ...

**Sir Gawain:** Because I broke my word!

*(Gawain takes off the belt. He looks at it sadly.)*

**Sir Gawain:** I kept the belt to save my life,
To my unending shame.
Farewell to Gawain's honour!
Farewell to my good name!
*(He puts the belt back on.)*

**The Minstrel:** The Green Knight disappeared – no one knows where – and Gawain rode sadly back to Arthur's court.

*(The Green Knight leaves the stage, and Jason takes away the Green Chapel scenery and replaces it with the scenery for Arthur's court. The knights and ladies of the court, Arthur and Guinevere come on and crowd round Gawain, very pleased to see him again.)*

**The Minstrel:** King Arthur and his court were overjoyed to see Gawain, as they had given him up for dead. Gawain told them everything that had happened to him. At first, some unkind knights made fun of him. But Arthur said he was sure none of them would have done better.

**King Arthur:** Gawain has sworn that he will wear
This belt, to show his shame.
So in his honour, I declare
We shall all do the same!

*(Knights and ladies bring on green belts which everyone takes and puts on so that they all look like a netball team.)*

**Guinevere:** And let us sing and dance with joy
To honour in this hall
Good Sir Gawain of Arthur's court,
The bravest knight of all!

*(Jason puts a tape on and the cast all sing and dance to the loudest piece of pop music they can find. Ms Clarke watches in open-mouthed astonishment for a few moments, and then climbs on to the stage, trying to get things under control.)*

**Ms Clarke:** Stop it! Stop it at once! What on earth are you doing? *(Screams)* Stop it!

*(Jason stops the tape. The cast all stop dancing.)*

**Ms Clarke:** *(With incredible patience)* What are you doing?

**Lee:** You said we had to do a dance at the end, Miss.

**Ms Clarke:** Not that kind of dance, for pity's sake, I meant an elegant dance. *(She does a few steps as the cast watch open-mouthed.)* The sort of dance they would have done in King Arthur's court ...

*(She realizes they are watching her in amazement, and is embarrassed.)*

**Ms Clarke:** Never mind, just take your bows and get off, go on ...

*(She claps determinedly as the cast take their bows and leave the stage. She turns to Mrs Phillips' chair.)*

**Ms Clarke:** Well, that didn't go too badly, did it? Just a few hiccups, but not too bad. I know the Green Knight and the Lord of the Castle are really the same person, but we thought it would be better to give two people parts, and anyway, Sam's make-up took so long to get on and off ...

**The Minstrel:** Miss ...

**Ms Clarke:** Yes, Sean?

**The Minstrel:** Mrs Phillips has gone, Miss.

*(Ms Clarke realizes that Mrs Phillips' chair is empty.)*

**Ms Clarke:** Oh, dear ... oh, dear ...

*(She starts to sniffle and wipes her eyes with a handkerchief.)*

**Guinevere:** *(Kindly)* Never mind, Miss. It'll be all right on the Green Knight.

*(Ms Clarke bursts into tears. The actors lead her away.)*

# Teachers' Notes

## Choosing Parts

The parts of Ms Clarke, the Minstrel, Sir Gawain, the Green Knight and the Lady of the Castle are the most demanding.

## Classroom Organization

The play has been designed to enable a whole class to take part in a reading. However, it may be more appropriate for a smaller group of children to read / act out the script. There are nine named speaking parts, but it would be easy for confident readers to take two roles. You could read the script through with the whole class before allowing a smaller group to act out the play. Alternatively, you could ask groups of different sizes to work on different scenes, before bringing the groups back as a whole class to put the play together.

## Putting On the Play

You may wish to put on a performance of the play, rather than just reading it. The following suggestions may provide you with a starting point for your own ideas about staging a production. Obviously, the use you make of these suggestions will vary depending on the time and resources available to your school.

**For permission to put on a profit-making performance of *Sir Gawain and the Green Knight*, please contact the Editorial Department, Ginn and Company, Prebendal House, Parson's Fee, Aylesbury, Bucks HP20 2QY.**
(There is no need to apply for permission if you are not charging an entrance fee, but please let us know if you are putting on any performance of this play, as we would be interested in hearing about it.)

### Staging

The play is divided into four scenes. All the scenes take place on a school stage. To bring out the fun of the 'play within a play', the scenery should look very amateurish. This could be achieved by using badly painted backdrops and badly made (or inappropriate) props and costumes.
*Scene 1* a chamber in King Arthur's Castle.
*Scene 2* a chamber in King Arthur's Castle, the Castle gate, the courtyard of the Lord's Castle.
*Scene 3* a chamber in the Lord's castle.
*Scene 4* the Green Chapel, a chamber in King Arthur's Castle.

### Costumes

**Ms Clarke** should be soberly dressed.
**The Knights** should wear tunics and tights.
**The Ladies** should wear long dresses and headdresses.
**The Minstrel** should have a jester's outfit.
**Sir Gawain** will need some form of armour for his journey.
The **Green Knight** will need a green costume.
The **Dragon's** costume could be made from a painted sheet and egg boxes.

### Props

Like the scenery, the props should have a 'home-made' feel. The following is a list of essential props:
*Scenes 1, 2, 4* Arthur's crown, a coconut shell.
*Scene 1* an axe, a sword, a green football with a head painted on it.
*Scene 2* a bush in a pot – the more withered, the better.
*Scene 3* foam antlers, green belts.

# Follow-up Work

## Research
Read some more stories about King Arthur and his knights. There are many retellings of the tales.

## Group Discussion
By the end of the play, Gawain is ashamed because he has broken his word.
- Why did he break his word?
- Has anyone in the class ever broken a promise?
- Why? What happened?
- Why do people tell lies?
- What happens when a person who has told a lie is found out?
- Has this happened to anyone in the class?

## Drama
### Hot-seating
Hot-seating is a strategy which can help pupils either to create a character or to develop a greater understanding of a character in the text.
1. Put a chair at the front of the class and arrange the rest of the class in a semi-circle around it.
2. Choose a child to represent one of the characters in the play, and ask him or her to sit in the hot seat.
3. The rest of the class must ask the child questions which he or she has to answer in role – in other words, as the character.
The object is to explore the character's motivation. You could hot seat any of the main characters in this way.

Although Mrs Phillips doesn't appear in the play, she could be hot-seated. You could ask her questions like:
- What did you think of the play?
- Will you allow it to be performed?
- Which were the worst bits of the play?
- Which were the best?
- Why don't you like drama?

### Rehearsed improvisation
After the children have read more adventures of Arthur and his knights, divide the class into groups of four or five and ask each group to produce a rehearsed improvisation of one of the stories. The sword in the stone episode or the death of Arthur and the returning of the sword Excalibur would be suitable.

## Artwork
Ask the children to draw or paint a poster for a production of *Sir Gawain and the Green Knight*. They should think carefully about the information they are trying to convey, and about how to make the poster eye-catching.